ARNOLD
AND
BESTWOOD
IN OLD PHOTOGRAPHS

THE OLD COUNCIL OFFICES. Front Street, built in 1875. Meetings were held in the upper rooms above the shop.

ARNOT HILL HOUSE, standing in the grounds of the worsted mill which was pulled down in 1811. It was extensively altered in the 1850s. Bought by the council for their new offices in 1914 for £3,700, its occupation was interrupted by the First World War. It was used until 1974, when, as a result of local government reorganization, Arnold became part of the Gedling borough and the offices were transferred to Carlton, but in 1985 the council returned to premises built in Arnot Hill Park which were paid for by the sale of the Carlton offices. The house is now used as an annex.

ARNOLD
AND
BESTWOOD
IN OLD PHOTOGRAPHS

—— COLLECTED BY ——
M.W. SPICK

ALAN SUTTON
Published in collaboration with

**Nottinghamshire County Council
Leisure Services**

Alan Sutton Publishing Limited
Phoenix Mill · Far Thrupp · Stroud · Gloucestershire

First published 1991

British Library Cataloguing in Publication Data

Arnold and Bestwood in old photographs.
I. Spick, M.W. (Maurice William)
942.528

ISBN 0-86299-954-5

Front Cover Illustration: ALL ABOARD FOR ARNOLD AND BESTWOOD, 1935. A year later trams
were replaced by buses and the fare rose from 3d. to 5d.

Typeset in 9/10 Korinna.
Typesetting and origination by
Alan Sutton Publishing Limited.
Printed in Great Britain by
The Bath Press, Avon.

CONTENTS

Whatever a place has to offer in terms of its heritage, its most important feature is those who have lived there and, by means of their labours, left a lasting influence on its history. This incomplete abbreviated list includes many who have helped me in my search for materials with which to illustrate Arnold's past.

ADAM Ruth, 1908–77, writer; ANNIBAL Thomas, 1875–1960, eccentric; AUSTIN 'Bunny', English footballer; BISHOP William, 1865–1959, policeman; BLANKLEY, family settled here in 1804, fourth and last member died in 1973; BETTISON Frederick, 1888–1959, County football player; BLUNT Benny, 1899–1974, an eccentric lovable character; CAVE Harold, OBE, d. 1986, local businessman and benefactor; COPE William, 1811–68, benefactor; CORAH Frederick, 1918–72, policeman and local football organizer; DOVE Samuel, 1863–1964, postmaster, councillor, an attempt was made on his life in 1934; DAFT John, founder member of Jessops of Nottingham; FARR Sydney, 1888–1967, member of Notts County Council and director of the Home Brewery and Laundry; HAMMOND Samuel, 1883–1955, businessman; HAWKESLEY Thomas, 1807–93, civil engineer; JAMES Mr, 1901–66, clerk to the council; JOHNSON William, d. 1963, born in Worksop, awarded VC in 1918; HOLCOMBE Francis, 1787–1872, vicar; JONES Cyril, 1916–72, awarded the American Silver Star in 1945; KIDDIER William, 1860–1934, artist who resided in Woodthorpe; KNIGHTON-HAMMOND, 1875–1965(?), artist; LEE L., b. 1922, raconteur; LOCKLEY Walter, 1889–1972, council affairs; McGUNN Ellen, 1889–1971, first woman chairman in 1957; MEE George, County footballer in the 1930s; MELLORS Robert, 1836–1931, education and local benefactor; PARKINSON Thomas, 1816–82, Methodist benefactor; PHIPPS Joseph, 1817–80, schoolmaster and benefactor, he finally committed suicide; POWLEY George, 1880–1960, farmer; ROBINSON John, 1839–1929, brewer and manufacturer, knighted in 1905; SAVILLE, 1815–44, when hanged for murder the crowd was so dense twelve people died in the crush; SEELY Charles, 1833–1915, benefactor, he built St Paul's church and Ramsdale House, knighted in 1896; SHIRTCLIFFE James, 1831–93, poet, preacher and benefactor; STACEY-BLAKE, 1873–1964, traveller and artist; STAREY T.R., 1819–91, coach builder and founder member of the Robin Hood Rifles; TINN Arnold, 1891–1962, meteorologist; WARDLEY William, 1911–90, football historian; WHITTAKER Joseph, 1799–1874, landowner and friend of royalty; WING D., b. 1905, motor cycle racer; WORRAL John, 1810–98, builder, farmer and tax collector; WRIGHT Allen, 1804–77, doctor, medical officer and benefactor.

INTRODUCTION

The stories of Arnold and Bestwood have been very closely associated throughout their histories. In 1086 lands in Arnold were allocated to Lenton and became part of Bestwood Lodge.

Before 1974 and incorporation into the Gedling Urban District it was about seven square miles in area, situated in a long valley running north and south, mainly to the east of the old road to the north (Mansfield Road). It was about five miles in length and up to a mile wide, on the northern outskirts of the city of Nottingham.

Arnold was mainly agricultural from its first record in the Domesday Book of 1086 until 1776 and the advent of industry. It was a parish increasingly burdened by lack of finance and the need to improve the lot of its inhabitants, a constant reminder of the evils the Industrial Revolution created.

Living standards deteriorated from the late eighteenth century, especially with the closing of the mill in 1811, and poor harvests led to general unrest. Life was at its lowest with the introduction of the workhouse as a result of the Poor Law Act of 1834. The state of the district came to public attention and, in response to a public enquiry, a Local Board was established in 1854.

Two years later the first photographs appeared.

SECTION ONE

Victorian Arnold

Glimpses of Arnold the last 100 Years,

BEING A LECTURE DELIVERED TO THE YOUNG MEN'S MUTUAL IMPROVEMENT SOCIETY OF THE GENERAL BAPTIST CHAPEL, ON SHROVE TUESDAY, 1859, AND AGAIN (BY REQUEST) EASTER MONDAY, APRIL 29, 1859.

There is nothing in the national or historical character of this village that furnishes matter for elaborate description. There are no isolated scenes of beauty in grove or valley; no calm majestic river to adorn and enliven the spacious landscape; no lofty mountain to fling down from its summit the golden splendours of the setting sun; no meandering streamlets nor sparkling cascades; no hoary, ivy-grown embattled heights, or ancient towers; nothing to furnish a song for the wandering minstrel; no tales of romantic adventure; no venerable shrines or saintly relics; no thrilling legends of baronial halls, or chivalrous knights; nor will the traveller be seen halting on his tour of research to linger beneath the shade of classic ruins, or gaze with astonishment upon some impressive monument of ancient grandeur. Yet there are scenes of pastoral beauty and rural verdure that please the lover of nature, and serve to impress on his mind the marks of human industry and civilization, combined with the wisdom and goodness of the Great Creator. With these preliminary remarks we proceed to give some details in the first place of the village itself.

DESCRIPTION.

It is supposed originally to have been called Docket, then Arnold, for Arnot Vale or Arnot Hill. As to

THE FIRST PAGE OF AN ARNOLD HISTORY published in 1875.

THIS IS BELIEVED TO BE A SKETCH OF ST MARY'S during restoration in 1870.

THE STONE PANEL UNDER THE CHURCH CLOCK has no authenticated record but is believed to represent the Annunciation.

A FARM ON FRONT STREET on the corner of Ravenswood Road in 1856. This is the earliest known photograph of the village.

FRONT STREET, 1900. The opening to the Croft, used for the wakes, is on the left and, in the distance, is the corner of Coppice Road where the Duke of St Albans offered to assist in setting up a market in 1886 which never materialized although a sign was fixed to the wall. All of these buildings have now vanished.

THE LOCAL PAWNSHOP in High Street.

THE ORPHANAGE, near Allen's Walk. It was erected in 1887 and demolished in the early 1920s.

Poor Uncle William of Arnold

At Nottingham Spring Races
The Arnold louts do say
That dear old Uncle William
Has lost his 'time of day.'

This is how it came about,
Just list to me I pray,
How Uncle William in the ring
Thus lost his 'time of day.'

He stood treat for a lady fair
In glasses two or three,
Until so kindly asked by her
What was the 'time of day.'

'Tis three o'clock me dear' says Bill,
Showing his ticker gay.
'The Handicap will now be rung
And that's the time of day.'

'Look there,' he cries. 'St Cuthbert wins.'
Ne'er one word did she say.
The false one did adsquatulate
With William's 'time of day'.

(*from* The Owl, *dated 10 May 1878*)

WEST STREET, adopted and named in 1876. Up until 1914 the Bin Bangers expressed their disapproval of any neighbours who stepped out of line by banging bin lids outside their home all day, hence their name.

ROBINSON'S YARD, one of many yards in the main thoroughfare area. It was the scene of Mrs Lambert and her family's murder.

REDHILL ARCH. The first bridge was built in 1815. This view, taken in 1860, is believed to show the original one.

THE HORSE AND JOCKEY INN. Front Street, the earliest known date of which is 1797. This photograph, taken in 1880, shows Tom Bailey, the driver of the coach, with his daughters either side of him, and Ted Bailey at the back.

KINGSWELL FARM, 1964. It derived its name from the curative waters of its spring. In medieval times the touch of the royal hand, like the practice of taking the waters, had been regarded as a cure for many ailments. The spring at this farm was so clear and pure that its fame grew, but there is no record of a royal visit.

THE VILLAGE SMITHY.

ADVERTISEMENTS.

Mr. MANN wishes to inform the public that he is not a cannibal, and to point out that there is an evident difference between a man eater and a Mann eating. The report is most unraisonable, and never ought to have become currant. A grocer calumny could not have been perpetrated, and he'll be jam'd if he'll stand it any longer.

Mr. GOSLING begs to say that he has given relief in many painful cases, and will be glad to do as much for all his friends.

Mrs. DICKINSON wishes her friends to know that her very fine Stone Ale is down from the wood.

Mr. WOOD begs to state that his best Mild Ales are always down from the stone.

Mr. WILLIAMSON respectfully states that his Bitter Beer is never sold now, as it has all good cellar-age.

Mr. DAN WARD is prepared to hang walls to any extent.

Mr. JOE begs to inform everybody that his New Bus will not run on the 2nd January, but his horse will, and the bus will follow shortly.

The DEAN humbly confesses that he is decidedly wrong in wearing an apron. He states, however, that when he becomes a cannon, he will certainly make breeches.

The CLAY BROTHERS assure the public that to the best of their knowledge they were not dug out of a pit. They were never kiln'd, and object to being called a pair of walking bricks. N.B.—The celebrated fur-long hosiery is not all made after a short nap.

A PAGE OF ADVERTS taken from a popular pamphlet called 'Punch and Judy's Visit to Arnold', Christmas 1881.

WELLINGTON STREET, one of the few roadways between Front and High Street. Sunderland Sue was to be found near here. Her family came down from the North looking for work in the mines during the 1930s. Following her husband's death she made herself very unpopular with those around her.

THE TRAVELLERS' REST was a popular walk away. It is recorded as far back as 1738.

CROSSLANDS FARM, Plains Road, 1920. Although not a Victorian photograph, this shows a rural area which has only recently been developed.

ARNOLD ACADEMY, 1860. This nineteenth-century school was run for many years by Joseph Phipps (born 1817), a tireless worker for the poor, until the strain proved too much and he committed suicide in 1880.

RURAL WOODTHORPE. The area looked like this until the First World War.

ARNOLD HILL HOUSE, one of the larger isolated houses.

The Parish Churches

ST MARY'S CHURCH, first noted in 1176, was rebuilt between 1315 and 1349. The tower was rebuilt in 1450. It was reconstructed between 1868 and 1871 and today has six bells. All the land in the photograph is now developed for housing and the Redhill Social Centre and School.

THE SEPULCHRE, ST MARY'S CHURCH. Although in poor condition, it is one of only four in the county.

A TEMPORARY ROOD SCREEN in St Mary's church in the 1920s.

REVD KING, vicar from 1907 to 1929. He was the co-producer of the *History of Arnold* in 1913.

THE CHURCH CHOIR.

THE GUIDES OF ST MARY'S CHURCH in 1941.

THE CHURCH FOOTBALL TEAM.

Church & Alms Houses, Daybrook, Nott's. Peveril Series.76

ST PAUL'S CHURCH, Daybrook, built between 1893 and 1895, was consecrated in 1896. The spire was added in 1897 and the almshouses in memory of Sandford Robinson opened in 1899. The church has eight bells.

ST PAUL'S CHURCH INTERIOR.

THE CRYPT OF LADY ROBINSON.

THE FIRST VICARAGE belonging to St Paul's church, and built at about the same time.

SCOUTS ON PARADE at Southwell, above, and in camp at Walesby in 1968, below. Their leader was Mr D. Orme.

WIVES' GROUPS, like this one at St Paul's church, were very influential.

ST PAUL'S FOOTBALL CLUB, 1911/12.

THE SUNDAY SCHOOL SPORTS was one of the many activities connected with St Paul's church. These photographs were taken in 1929.

ST MARK'S CHURCH, Woodthorpe, designed by R.W. Cooper and costing £45,000, was built in 1962 and consecrated in 1964.

THE INTERIOR OF ST MARK'S CHURCH, Woodthorpe, 1964.

The War Years

THE BARRACKS, REDHILL, named after the recruits for the wars billeted here before leaving.

PEACE.

News reached London on Sunday evening June 1 that the terms of Peace had been signed.

Great rejoicing took place as the news became known all over the country.

GREAT RELIEF AND JOY WAS FELT when this leaflet was freely distributed in Arnold in 1902 at the end of the Boer War.

A SINISTER VISITOR photographed from Kingswell Farm in 1916.

THE DRILL HALL, Arnot Hill Road, was opened on 2 May 1914 by Colonel Mellish.

CROWDS WATCH THE OPENING OF THE DRILL HALL.

ARNOT HILL PARK became an auxiliary hospital at the outbreak of the First World War, shortly after it had been acquired by the Council. A nurse feeds 'Old Jack', the swan.

THE NURSING STAFF at Arnot Hill Park, 1914.

A PAINFUL EXPERIENCE!

BELGIAN REFUGEES who settled here at the end of the First World War.

A VOLUNTEER GROUP in 1914.

THE WHIT WALK in 1917. Even war did not stop it.

NOTTINGHAM ROAD. A firing range was established here for a time.

CARNEGIE LIBRARY, built in 1906. This view, taken in 1925, shows the roll of honour of those who fell in the First World War.

THE CORNER OF MANSFIELD AND ST ALBAN'S ROAD. The white building was at various times a blouse factory, a doll factory and, during the Second World War, used for services to the military. All the other property has recently been moved for road widening and the factory is now vacant.

Issued by the Ministry of   Information on behalf of
the War Office and the Ministry of Home Security

STAY WHERE YOU ARE

IF this island is invaded by sea or air everyone who is not under orders must stay where he or she is. This is not simply advice: it is an order from the Government, and you must obey it just as soldiers obey their orders. Your order is "Stay Put", but remember that this does not apply until invasion comes.

Why must I stay put?

Because in France, Holland and Belgium, the Germans were helped by the people who took flight before them. Great crowds of refugees blocked all roads. The soldiers who could have defended them could not get at the enemy. The enemy used the refugees as a human shield. These refugees were got out on to the roads by rumour and false orders. Do not be caught out in this way. Do not take any notice of any story telling what the enemy has done or where he is. Do not take orders except from the Military, the Police, the Home Guard (L.D.V.) and the A.R.P. authorities or wardens.

What will happen to me if I don't stay put?

If you do not stay put you will stand a very good chance of being killed. The enemy may machine-gun you from the air in order to increase panic, or you may run into enemy forces which have landed behind you. An official German message was captured in Belgium which ran:

(' Watch for civilian refugees on the roads. Harass them as much as possible.''

Our soldiers will be hurrying to drive back the invader and will not be able to stop and help you. On the contrary, they will

THE REALITY OF WAR was really brought home with the fear of imminent invasion in 1940. Arnold's main defence was E Coy, 5th Notts Home Guard. In order to keep the home fires burning Mr Stacey, now living in Costock, organized many events and, as an air raid official, recalls a night in 1940 when the alert was sounded of parachutes falling in the area; it turned out to be barrage balloons at the Rolls-Royce works in Derby. A miner coming off duty at Gedling Colliery was nearly shot as he had no identity card but was too petrified to explain why.

A RED CROSS GROUP, 1914. Ready for any emergency, they were led by Dr Francis (in the white coat).

HAMMONDS GARAGE (founded in 1905) was requisitioned and used as a fire station in the Second World War. It was not handed back until 1949.

ARNOLD ENTERTAINS THE CREW OF THE CORVETTE HMS *PENNYWORT* which it had adopted in the Second World War.

FEEDING THE CHILDREN ON WEST STREET. This probably shows a VJ celebration party.

WOMEN WAR WORKERS.

ARNOLD'S MOBILE POLICE on Redhill Road in 1939.

VJ CELEBRATIONS ON RAVENSWOOD ROAD.

VJ PARTY ON JAMES STREET.

Royal Progress

THE CORONATION of King George V and Queen Mary is celebrated by this patriotic group gathered outside the Baptist church in Front Street. Royalty has travelled through the area from early times to the nearby Bestwood Royal Forest and up the Mansfield Road to the north. The first royal visitor to actually visit was the Princess Alexandra on 21 October 1983.

THE ROYAL CAR stops for loyal greetings in 1914.

MORE PEOPLE GREET THE ROYAL VISITORS near the almshouses in 1914.

THE ROYAL VISIT, 1928. Crowds look on as King George V and Queen Mary leave the city of Nottingham, following a visit there, and enter Arnold.

THE PRINCE OF WALES PASSES BY. In 1929 the Prince of Wales (later Edward VII) opened the new Council House in Nottingham then travelled north to stay at one of the grand houses in the Dukeries.

ALICE PARR AND DONKEY SAYWELL celebrate the coronation of King George VI and Queen Elizabeth.

COUNCILLOR J.E. CLARKE AND MRS E.M. CLARKE, Mayor and Mayoress of Gedling, being presented to HM the Queen at County Hall on the occasion of her Silver Jubilee in 1977.

Dark Satanic Mills

ALLEN SOLLY'S PREMISES, Brookfield Road in 1955. The factory system was introduced into Arnold in the late 1870s.

ALLEN SOLLY of Brookfield Road started in business in 1888. An earlier Allen was indentured in the area in 1744.

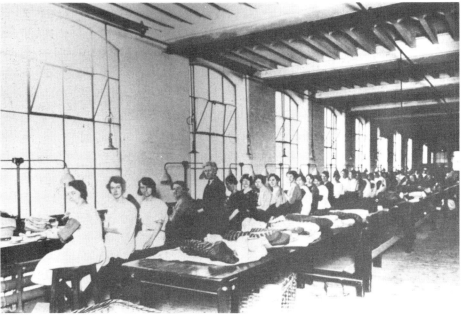

THE FINISHING ROOM.

THE WINDING ROOM. This series of photographs is believed to have been taken in the 1920s.

THE LINK AND SEAM ROOM.

JACOBY'S FACTORY, Sherbrook Road in 1884. It was sold to a consortium of small firms in 1934. A fire in 1913 caused £20,000 worth of damage; another in 1939 cost £100,000.

THE SHELL OF JACOBY'S after the fire of 1913. In the House of Commons praise was given to the newly formed fire brigade.

A FACTORY INTERIOR WORK ROOM.

THE SOUTH AMERICAN DEPARTMENT.

THE WINDING ROOM.

A SECOND FIRE, in 1939, caused £100,000 worth of damage.

I. & R. MORLEY expanded from Nottingham in 1874 and lasted until 1963.

THE SORTING AND OVERLOCKING ROOM.

THE DIRECTORS of I. & R. Morley in the 1930s.

A CHRISTMAS PARTY in 1941.

DAYBROOK LAUNDRY AND RECEPTION OFFICE.

THE DRYING AREA, 1905.

THE DIRECTORS photographed in the 1920s.

THE DRY CLEANING DEPARTMENT.

THE INTERIOR OF THE LAUNDRY, 1905.

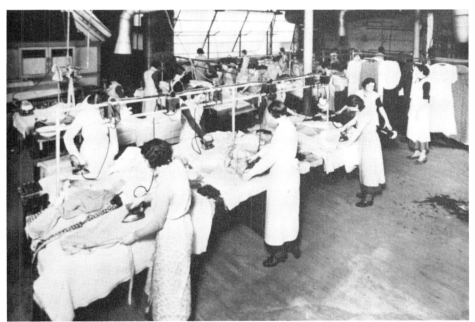

THE INTERIOR, 1905.

THE ANNUAL OUTING TO THE SEA.

SOME OF THE OFFICE STAFF ON THE OUTING.

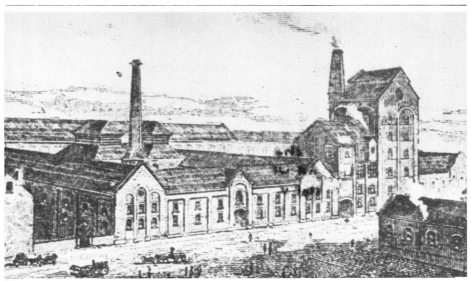

THE HOME BREWERY, 1883. This shows the works as seen from Portland Street.

THE OLD AND THE NEW HOME BREWERY.

LOCAL LICENSEES enjoying a day's outing to the home of Sir John Robinson at Worksop Manor.

One Religion – Many Faiths

Foundation Stone laid Feb. 28th, 1865, by SAMUEL MORLEY, ESQ., M.P.   Opening Sermon Preached Aug. 29th, 1865, by the REV. [...]
Public Meeting, presided over by CHARLES PAGET, ESQ.   Architect, MR. JOHN COLLYER; Builders, MR. JOHN WOOLLEY, and Mr. [...]

THE METHODIST CHURCH, FRONT STREET. The first Methodists arrived in 1790. The manager of the mill in Arnot Hill Park had the Old Council Yard building erected to teach the children. This building was erected in 1865 and named the Ebenezer, which means Stone of Help. During 1943 the schoolroom was used as a British restaurant.

EBENEZER CHURCH INTERIOR.

EBENEZER CHURCH CHOIR. Mrs Radford, the conductor, is fifth from the left in the second row.

THE PRIMITIVE METHODIST CHURCH, HIGH STREET, first erected in 1829, was enlarged between 1876 and 1886 and demolished in 1967.

HARVEST FESTIVAL at the Primitive Methodist church, a popular and well attended event.

THE PRIMITIVE METHODIST CHOIR. The lady at front left is Miss Betty Hall, who received the Maundy Money at Southwell in 1984.

AN OUTING FROM THE HIGH STREET METHODIST CHURCH.

THE WESLEYAN CHURCH ON CHURCH DRIVE, built in 1900, was bought by the God of Prophecy in 1969.

WESLEYAN CHURCH INTERIOR.

THE WESLEYAN FOOTBALL TEAM in 1923.

MR HARPER sitting at the rear of Library House. He was the local librarian. A breakaway Methodist Group met in the buildings behind between 1867 and 1879.

THE NEW METHODIST CHURCH was built to unite all three Methodist movements under the leadership of the Revd K. Cupit. The stained glass window above the communion table was donated by Miss L. Hall in 1968.

THE CROSS ON THE METHODIST CHURCH, originally placed on St Bartholomew's church, Woodborough Road, Nottingham, was given to the Methodist church in Arnold in 1974.

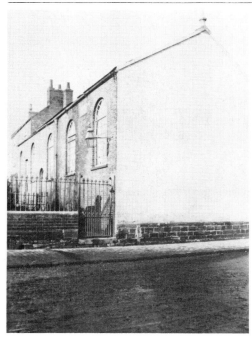

THE FIRST BAPTIST CHURCH stood on Front Street between 1840 and 1883.

THE INTERIOR OF FRONT STREET BAPTIST CHURCH.

A HAPPY OCCASION in the Baptist church, Front Street.

FRONT. ST. BAPTIST.

A FRONT STREET BAPTIST CHURCH DECORATED DRAY.

THE BAPTIST CHURCH stood on Daybrook Square between 1844 and 1908. In 1899 a breakaway movement transferred to Redhill.

THE DAYBROOK BAPTIST CHURCH INTERIOR.

A DAYBROOK BAPTIST CHARABANC OUTING.

RED.HILL.BAPTIST "1ST.PRIZE".

THE REDHILL BAPTIST CHURCH DECORATED DRAY.

AN EARLY VIEW of the interior of the Cross Street Baptist chapel.

THE INTERIOR OF THE CROSS STREET
BAPTIST CHAPEL.

CROSS STREET BAPTISTS assembling for the Whit Walk outside their church.

GOING TO ASSEMBLE ON THE REC.

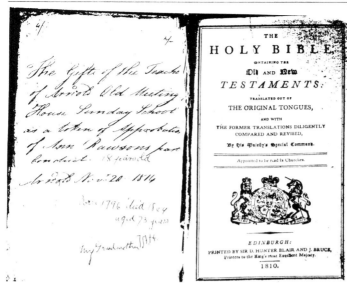

AN UNUSUAL FLY LEAF ENTRY in an old bible. The early meetings of Cross Street Baptists were in Meeting House Yard. Ann Rowson appears to have been a devoted worker. Her father was master of the Free School.

ROMAN CATHOLICS first met in Coppice Road in 1922, then at a factory near the railway bridge, and in 1929 built this church on Thackerays Lane. Later a very modern enlargement was built and today there is a chapel-of-ease on Shirley Drive as well as three schools in the area.

As well as the Methodist and Baptist faiths in the parish, other active nonconformists were, with their earliest dates: the Congregationalists (1870), Wesleyan Reform (1894), Christian Spiritualists (1930), Jehovah's Witnesses (1943), the Assembly of God (1951) and the Church of the God of Prophecy in 1969. Active in the area since 1880, the Salvation Army met at the bottom of Coppice Road (then Spout Lane) until 1932 when they bought and furbished premises (now the Assembly of God church) on Furlong Street for £295, which were opened by Mr W. Harlow. Apparently, these premises were a small bobbin factory which it was stipulated when sold were only to be used for religious purposes.

Whit Walk

THE WHIT WALK, believed to have begun as a religious festival, was taken over by the Lodges then transferred to the Sunday schools, the earliest of which began in 1858. Popular in times of adversity, it was to become the major event of the year until the rapid growth of the town created insurmountable obstacles and it ended in 1977.

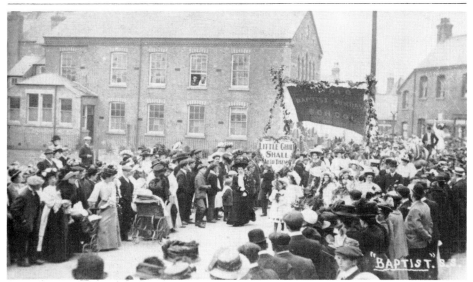

ASSEMBLING OUTSIDE THE EBENEZER.

A HALT AT THE TOP O' THE TOWN.

ONLOOKERS IN DAYBROOK SQUARE.

ST MARY'S GROUP JOINS IN.

THE WHIT WALK of 1917.

THIS PHOTOGRAPH is believed to be of the first Whit Walk Parade on the Rec.

THE WHIT WALK has begun with an opening service on the bottom rec since 1925.

WHILE THE SERVICE WAS ON, the decorated lorries and floats were judged in the nearby streets. (Note the spelling mistake on the back of the lorry.)

A FLOAT ON HIGH STREET, near Bonnington House.

THE CHURCH DRIVE METHODISTS' EFFORT.

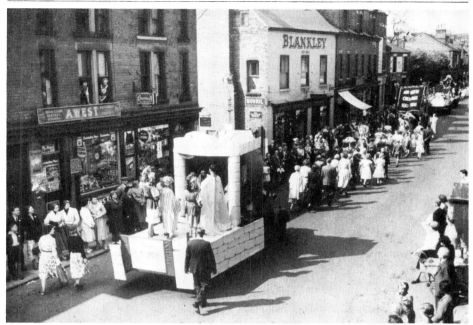

WHIT PARADE on Front Street near Blankley's shop.

THE PARADE on High Street. A new hat was a must for the ladies.

THE WHIT WALK at the height of its popularity.

Ikepimatompikingtatas

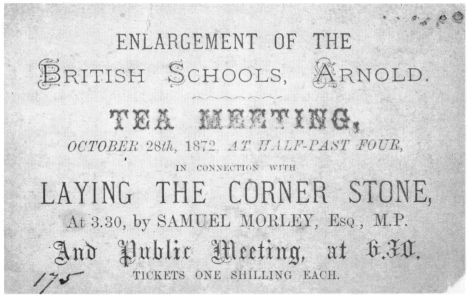

ENLARGEMENT OF THE
BRITISH SCHOOLS, ARNOLD.

TEA MEETING,

OCTOBER 28th, 1872, AT HALF-PAST FOUR,

IN CONNECTION WITH

LAYING THE CORNER STONE,

At 3.30, by SAMUEL MORLEY, Esq., M.P.

And Public Meeting, at 6.30.

TICKETS ONE SHILLING EACH.

FUND RAISING FOR THE BRITISH SCHOOL IN FRONT STREET. The year 1870 seems to have been a watershed year for the development of modern Arnold. Factory life created a need for better educated workers. A charity school had been founded in 1701 but during the eighteenth century only the privileged could attend the boarding school. Simple education had been given by nonconformists during the early part of the nineteenth century to help children understand the bible and other religious texts. The Education Act provoked mixed reactions in the village, mainly because of the loss of the money children could earn, and many excuses were found – such as that used for the title of this section – to avoid attending. By 1891 attendance was compulsory and free, and up until the First World War permission had to be sought for children leaving early and then only if a certain standard had been reached.

HIGH STREET SCHOOL. College Street was closed to the public in 1967.

A HIGH STREET INFANT SCHOOL CLASS of the Edwardian period.

MR A. HIGGINBOTTOM was headmaster of the British School, Front Street.

A DAYBROOK SCHOOL CLASS photographed at the end of the First World War.

MR S. SPENCER, headmaster of the British School on Front Street. This was set up in the late nineteenth century to rival the Church of England school which had been established on Calverton Road in 1860.

THE BONNINGTON STATUE, erected in 1911 outside the School of Art, Nottingham. Bonnington was born on High Street, Arnold where his mother had a boarding school, and is considered one of the founders of the English School of painting.

THE BRITISH SCHOOL AT DAYBROOK lasted from 1879 to 1961.

A CLASS AT DAYBROOK SCHOOL in 1926.

A DAYBROOK SCHOOL CLASS of 1898.

ST ALBAN'S SCHOOL, opened in 1961.

THE CLASS OF 1893 at the British School, Front Street. The boy second from left in the front row was Mr Blankley, the chemist.

A DAYBROOK SCHOOL CLASS PHOTOGRAPH taken in the annexe yard at the Baptist church in 1960.

AN ARNO VALE SCHOOL TEAM of 1937.

OXCLOSE LANE was made a dual carriageway during 1968 and many arguments concerning safety were voiced before it was decided to build a bridge crossing.

SECTION NINE

People and Places

COTTAGE ROW, DAYBROOK. Built in 1790 to house one thousand mill workers, it was converted to houses in 1815. Catty Nan, a local eccentric, lived in No. 12. What was considered the finest industrial building in the area was demolished in 1968.

A SERIES OF WALL SKETCHES were found at No. 2 and are believed to have been made by the last constable elected by the vestry (before the modern police force came into being) when he lived there. The photograph is of Mrs Eddyshaw showing them to a friend.

AN EIGHTEENTH-CENTURY OVEN discovered under No. 1 Cottage Row when it was being demolished. It was filled in and left.

PENDINE HOUSE, home of Brough the cycle inventor from 1932 to 1970. Among his visitors were Lawrence of Arabia and, it is said, George Bernard Shaw.

MR BLANKLEY, who died in 1973, the last of four generations to control the chemists, seed merchants and wine merchants business since it began in 1804. In 1885, after a disastrous fire which caused £5,000 worth of damage, the Duke of St Albans wrote to Mr Blankley asking him to thank the people of Arnold for not taking advantage of the confusion to cause further damage or take anything!

SCATTERGOODS WERE A LOCAL FIRM. This was their first lorry, driven by Mr Scragg.

FLOODS ON BROOKFIELD ROAD, 1951. Flooding was a constant problem for the parish.

RAMSDALE HOUSE, Dorket Head, built by Sir C. Seely in 1907, was used as a school in the Second World War. It became a special school in 1950 before being converted to a home for the physically disabled.

NO. 34 HIGH STREET, one of the three oldest buildings in the area.

MOIRA HOUSE, Front Street, built for a former viceroy of India. It was the home of the local doctors from 1865 until just before its demolition in 1976.

THE LOCAL SWEEP in 1920.

SHERWOOD LODGE, built in 1790, was the home of Revd Holcombe, a 'squireson', for many years. 'Squireson' is a local name for a vicar who chooses to live like the squire of the village. Revd Holcombe was a real despot and the longest serving vicar (1812–1872) in the parish. The Lodge was bought by the police for £100,000 in 1973 and demolished shortly after. The new County Headquarters were opened in 1979.

THE TENANTS OF SHERWOOD LODGE in 1890.

A POPULAR OUTING was to 'Jonah's', situated near the bottom of Somersby Road.

INSPECTOR HORNSEY was policeman, poet and helper of the underprivileged.

WATERLOO COTTAGES, Calverton Road, built in the year of, and named after the battle, are now demolished.

SWINEHOUSE FARM, WOODTHORPE. At the turn of this century it was occupied by the Chambers family. Jessie was the lover of D.H. Lawrence and he visited her there. In *Sons and Lovers* he called it Swineshead.

KITTY, born in 1945, lived to a great age. She is seen with her keeper and groom, Mr W. Bleazard, a real personality.

MUSIC was a great relief and pleasure. The Arnold Band and Albion Prize Band were great favourites.

Time for Leisure

IN THE LATTER PART OF THE NINETEENTH CENTURY shorter working hours were introduced by law for the first time. With the arrival of the railway and, later, road transport the public's horizons were broadened. Daybrook railway station was built in 1875. The Suburban Line joined it in 1889. Both were closed in 1960.

THE RAILWAY BRIDGE AT DAYBROOK SQUARE. Locals always say they knew they were home when it came into view. Sadly it disappeared in 1966.

A 'SPECIAL' APPROACHING DAYBROOK in 1951. The road at the top is Woodthorpe Drive. The Marlborough Road and Thackerays Lane bridges were demolished in 1973.

A TRIP TO THE SEASIDE — with proper decorum at all times — was made possible by public transport.

THERE WAS GREAT EXCITEMENT when pneumatic tyres appeared in 1906.

THE BLACK SWANN INN, 1808–1912(?). This was the first and last pub in the village.

FRONT STREET. The building on the right was known as the New Inn from 1893 to 1932.

BULWELL FIELDS, a popular walk, even though it led to the workhouse (now Highbury Hospital).

JACOB'S LADDER, Edwards Lane was a very popular walk. The people on it are Mr Hensey and Mr Dove with his two children.

THE LADIES' FOOTBALL TEAM in 1921 raised thousands of pounds to help the distressed. The names are, back row, left to right: Easom sen., Holmes, Holbrooke, Williamson, D. Smith, Blunt, M. Smith, A. Eaton, Rattenbury, Prior. Middle row: Jackson, Marriott, Annabel, Beardsley, Abbott, Foster, Casterton, Pembleton, Anthony, F. Easom, Fell, Subden. Front row: Cook, Cooling, Woodward, D. Rattenbury, Kelly, Fisher, Sansome, Williamson, Needham, Fountain, Harrison.

A SPECIAL TREAT for the poor children of Arnold in the 1920s.

ORIGINALLY BUILT AS THE ST ALBAN'S THEATRE and opened in 1912, the Bonnington Cinema was rebuilt in 1929. It closed in 1957.

NEW EMPRESS, Front Street. Opened in 1912, it became a dance hall and shop before demolition. To the left stands Rowbottoms, the butchers since 1908.

A WINTER SCENE in Woodthorpe Drive (formerly Scout Lane). The building is the old toll-house.

A BUS AT THE TOP OF BRECKHILL ROAD in the 1950s. This photograph clearly shows how the parish lies in a valley.

THIS CRICKET TEAM, C. 1890, at the flower show in Robinson's Field included, standing: Ellis, Stenhouse, Askew, -?-, Holbrook, Sissons, -?-, Varley, Showell, -?-, Jew, Bush, Sutton, Nicholson, Finnucan. Seated: Oscroft, Foster, Dove, Bailey, Robinson, Parr (captain), Truman, Franks, Stenhouse, Clay, Handley, Powley. Front row: Worton, Sanders, -?-, Ellis, -?-, Coupe, Clay. At the left end, wearing the trilby hat, is Wright Ellis.

A CRICKET TEAM OF ABOUT 1950.

THE CRICKET TEAM of the 1950s.

'OKEY POKEY, PENNY A LUMP.' An ice cream street vendor near Salop Street, 1938.

SIMPLE RECREATIONS, like dressing up, are still popular with youngsters.

EVEN THE OLDER FOLK ENJOYED DRESSING UP FOR A PURPOSE.

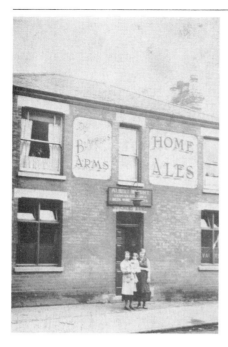

THE BUTCHER'S ARMS, Front Street, 1935. Mr Wright was the landlord then, and his family ran the pub for many years.

WOMEN'S LIB. in 1893.

A RARE MOMENT OF LEISURE was a privilege for this careworn Edwardian housewife.

A LIBERATED LADY of the 1930s.

ARNOLD RANGERS FC, 1921.

EVENING SCHOOL FC.

A LOCAL FOOTBALL TEAM at Calverton Road School.

G. GOODHEAD, a well-known footballer.

AN OLD ARNOLD FOOTBALL TEAM of the 1899/1900 season.

VETERAN FOOTBALLERS of the 1920s. They are, from left to right: Lockley, Hearson, Gwatkin, Whitt, Mountain, Briggs, Rhodes, Rockley, Pinket, Rose, Cooke, Langford, Peck, Annabel, Scott, Gee, Lomas, Archer and Goadsby.

THE CALL OF THE ROAD in 1920. There were thirty-four tours to choose from in this brochure.

ARNOLD LICENSEES AT WORKSOP MANOR.

EVEN THE LOCAL POLITICIANS ENJOYED A DAY OUT but it is not known where they went.

ARNOLD COUNCIL VISITS WORKSOP MANOR.

OUT FOR THE AFTERNOON IN GRAND STYLE. It is not known of whom or where this photograph was taken but the date is believed to be 1946.

AN OUTING from the Vale Hotel for customers and friends in 1939.

OTHER GROUPS ENJOYED A DAY IN DERBYSHIRE. This one was organized by Mrs Price, a local music teacher who died in 1968.

'Modern Times'

FRONT STREET AT THE TURN OF THE CENTURY. Before 1876 it was known as Main Street, Town Street and Church Street as well as Front Street. Well-known businesses still extant include Chambers (since 1899) and Rowbottoms (since 1908).

A ROUND ENGLAND AIR RACE lands at Dorket Head, 28 July 1911.

THE WAKES was an annual event killed off by progress in 1963.

DAYBROOK SQUARE, showing the old post office and the Grove Inn, in existence since 1860. The hamlet of Daybrook grew around 1790 with the arrival of the new mill. Unfortunately, relationships with local people were soured by the mill owners' interfering with the rights of way at the junction of the road to Arnold. They also provided their own labour from other sources. After the mill closed in 1811 the area was known as The Folly for many years.

SALOP STREET in 1913, still very rural in appearance. On the left is the laundry chimney, on the right, in the distance, Jacoby's factory chimney.

MANSFIELD ROAD, Daybrook in the mid-1930s.

A RARE AERIAL VIEW, dated 1908 and taken from the Home Brewery tower, which clearly shows the public cemetery and the rural surroundings on the west side of Arnold.

NO. 68 MANSFIELD ROAD, DAYBROOK was originally laid out as a mini-park. Children who misbehaved were threatened with the crocodiles in the lake. The house was used as a centre for midwives, and is now used for private business. A small entrance on Church Drive was known as the 'kissing gate'.

THE OLD SPOT INN in 1928. It can trace its history back to 1784.

MANSFIELD ROAD IN DAYBROOK — known as Sloethorn, a reminder of the profusion of berries which grew here.

HAMMOND'S GARAGE. Founded in 1905, it was closed during the Second World War and remained so until 1949 when the phenomenal growth we know today was engineered by Mr T.E. Parr. In May 1978 it was taken over by the Greater Nottingham Co-operative Society.

THE WHITE HART, built about 1765, was demolished in 1964 and new premises built behind it.

OSBORNE COTTAGES, Mansfield Road, Redhill, since demolished for modern development.

MANSFIELD ROAD, REDHILL. This hamlet developed around 1800 with the improvements in transport and the need for a staging post before the road entered Sherwood Forest. It hung on tenaciously to its early independence.

IRISHMAN'S COTTAGE, REDHILL.

REDHILL. For many years the shape of the road and the many pubs here created problems – in 1903 there was a dispute over an increase in the price of a pint of beer and, through strike action, the customers won.

REDHILL ARCH was built when the road was first lowered to gain access to the farms and water reservoir. This is the second bridge.

REDHILL, known as the 'Rede Rode' since 1218. It was here that the great forest of Sherwood began. The Guide House on the left was demolished in 1978. Its history could be traced back to 1562.

QUEEN STREET, formerly known as 'Pig Tod Alley'.

WALTER'S YARD. CHURCH STREET was the birthplace of George Mee, the county footballer.

FRONT STREET, LEADING TO CHURCH STREET.

ANOTHER YARD OFF FRONT STREET. This is believed to be Stansfield Yard.

TOM TURNER'S, begun in 1911. The shop, on the east side of Front Street, was demolished to make way for a superstore. Turner moved further up the street on the opposite side.

THIS VIEW, taken in 1915, shows the Empress Cinema, opened in 1912, Packers Shop and Corner in the centre and the Baptist chapel on the right. The cemetery is under the tree.

FRONT STREET, nowadays completely altered and pedestrianized. When this photograph was taken in 1920 the British School stood at the right of the church. It was eventually demolished and replaced by the market. To the left of the church was Worrall Avenue, at the side of which the Whit Parades used to assemble – where the Labour Exchange and post office now stand. In medieval times this was the site of the second manor of Arnold.

FRONT STREET, 1920. High Street was on the left. The lamp was popularly known as the Christmas lamp. Most of the property has gone or been modernized and the road is pedestrianized. The junction is now grandly called The Green.

FRONT STREET PROPERTY which was removed to make way for Sainsburys' premises.

THE OPENING OF CARNEGIE LIBRARY, 1906.

JOHNSON'S SHOP. High Street. Note the variety of goods for sale.

R. MELLORS UNVEILING THE BONNINGTON PLAQUE on 26 October 1929. The Labour Party had used the house as its headquarters since 1909.

HIGH STREET, more popularly known as Back Side (meaning the back way). It acquired its official title in 1876.

CROSS STREET, 1960.

FURLONG STREET. It is not known why the road was reduced to a 'twitchell' (a name peculiar to this area).

ST ALBAN'S ROAD, formerly known as Broadmere Lane, another of the roads whose name was changed in 1876.

JEW'S JOINERY BUSINESS in Arnot Hill Road was founded in 1840 and has now transferred to Catton Road, Rolleston Drive Complex.

HALLAMS LANE. Sainsburys now stands on this site.

FLOODS ON HALLAMS LANE in 1947.

NOTTINGHAM ROAD. Mr H. Cave, standing outside his business, was a founder member of the OAP Centre.

PORTLAND STREET, 1957, with Magdala Square was the poorest area in the parish and had the last back to back houses.

SECTION TWELVE

Epilogue

THE FINAL JOURNEY. Although the church of St Mary's graveyard was extended, it eventually became so full that a new solution had to be found. The problem was resolved when the 10th Duke of St Albans offered four acres of land on the western side of Mansfield Road. The new cemetery was opened in 1879 and divided equally between the church and nonconformists; designed by R.E. Clarke of Nottingham, the total cost was £3,000.

MONUMENTAL REMEMBRANCES FOR LOVED ONES were made here by Hodsons at Daybrook.

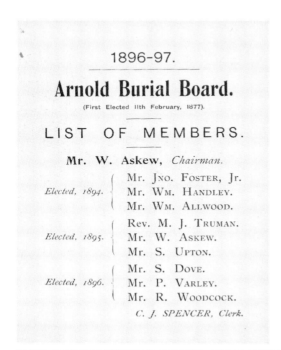

1896-97.

Arnold Burial Board.

(First Elected 11th February, 1877).

LIST OF MEMBERS.

Mr. W. Askew, *Chairman.*

Elected, 1894.
- Mr. JNO. FOSTER, JR.
- Mr. WM. HANDLEY.
- Mr. WM. ALLWOOD.

Elected, 1895.
- Rev. M. J. TRUMAN.
- Mr. W. ASKEW.
- Mr. S. UPTON.

Elected, 1896.
- Mr. S. DOVE.
- Mr. P. VARLEY.
- Mr. R. WOODCOCK.

C. J. SPENCER, Clerk.

A COUNCIL NOTICE of 1896/7.

THE ORIGINAL CEMETERY opened in 1879 and was divided equally between the Church of England and the nonconformists. It was controlled by the council from 1916.

THE CEMETERY TODAY, the public clock from the Ebenezer church being placed on the tower. It extended to over 25 acres by the end of 1990 and there were 23,524 interred in the grounds. Strangely, today one has to conduct business through the recreation department of the council!

THE CEMETERY SPIRE was struck by lightning on 28 February 1967.

THE FUNERAL of Mrs Lambert and her three children, who were murdered in Robinson's Yard in 1909. Matilda Lambert, 27, and her children, John, 8, Annie, 5, and Samuel, 2, were murdered on 12 July by S. Atherley, aged 35, who stunned them then cut their throats before unsuccessfully turning the razor on himself. Atherley was found guilty of the crime on 13 November and executed at Bagthorpe Prison on 14 December.

THE FUNERAL PROCESSION of Sir John Robinson, 1929. The Robinson family came to live in Arnold in the early part of the nineteenth century. Thomas, who farmed 1,000 acres of land, was also maltster, woolstapler and brickyard owner. He had two sons — Samuel, and John who was born in 1839. John bought the Home Brewery site and quickly established the brewery; his brother founded the laundry. John was knighted in 1905 and died in 1929 at Worksop Manor which he had purchased in 1890.

SWEET KATE OF ARNO VALE.

Let courtiers sigh for beauties high,
　Who flaunt in rich brocade;
No borrowed charms my bosom warms,
　I love a country maid.
The bloom that glows upon her cheeks
　Might make the rose look pale,
But richer charms adorn the mind
　Of Kate of Arno Vale.

Her modest smiles and gentle mein,
　Serenest joys impart;
And every look and word display
　Her pure and loving heart.
Her mother's eyes with rapture beam
　When love and hope prevail,
Because she knows that truth adorns
　Sweet Kate of Arno Vale.

The cot in which my fathers dwelt,
　With rural plenty stored,
Will soon possess whate'er I wish
　When Kate adorns my board.
Her gentle voice to me will sound
　Like music on the gale;
And oh! what bliss, her lips to kiss,
　Sweet Kate of Arno Vale.

THE MAID OF ARNO'S DEAD.

BY SAMUEL MULLENS.

The rosebud droops in Arno Vale,
　The lily hangs its head;
A mournful tale swells on the gale,
　"The Maid of Arno's dead!"
Twelve maidens bright, in virgin white,
　Her early death bewail,
As slowly to her grave they bear
　The Maid of Arno Vale.

The light that trembled in her eye,
　The bloom her features wore,
May wake affection's fondest sigh,
　But will not charm us more.
There's silence in her mother's cot;
　Alas! how changed the tale!
Her merry voice made all rejoice;
　Sweet Maid of Arno Vale.

Yet she was lovely in her death,
　And like a flower exhaled;
No passion wild her breast defiled,
　Where hope and peace prevailed.
Light on her heart the turf shall lie,
　And fragrance load the gale
Where lilies wave above her grave,
　The Maid of Arno Vale.

THE STORY OF A LOCAL CELEBRITY, written by Samuel Mullens and published in 'The Old Sailor's Jolly Boat' in 1877.

ST MARY'S CHURCHYARD was tidied up in 1978 and all but a few of the stones removed. This one is now the oldest, naming Mary Leadbeter who died in 1716 aged 56 years.

Bestwood

A carved stone weighing 4 cwt and telling the story of Bestwood was erected in the Lodge grounds at the side of the fountain in 1910. Damaged during the Second World War by the troops, it suddenly went missing in 1983 only to turn up later in a private house in Arnold.

*Here to the south of old Sherwood
Once a royal pleasance stood,
Hunting lodge and bower discreet
Of our king's plantaganet,
At their will to war or woo
(Since no wrong a king may do)
Each with his unlicensed dame.*

*Here our joyous Edward came,
And here lies too a king no less
Of the greenwood's fastnesses,
Robin Hood who roamed and ran
The king's deer with Marian.*

*See the buck leap round us yet
In their testimony set,
Kings are outlaws, outlaws king
In the court of carnal things.
Thus of old behold anon*

*Martyred Charles's royal son
Came with Mistress Eliner,
Granted Bestwood for her bower.
Came she here in widowed state,
Mourning yet most consolate.*

*In her offspring that Beauclerk
Wed to heiress of De Vere,
Nell's first son through whom we trace
Our St Alban's ducal race,
Still its lords. Time rambles on.
Of the hunting lodge no stone
You may find but this plain house
Built by one more virtuous
Than the most of them who made
Their brief sojourn in its shade.
Drop no tear for it or me.
Rather since Times' kings are we
Laugh an hour with me and these,
Soon to join them in their peace.*

(W.B., 1910)

BESTWOOD PARK FROM ARNOLD LANE, 1918. The row of trees curving in the centre is now Beckhampton Road. The farm on the right is Sunrise Hill Farm.

THE POSTMAN, nicknamed Porky, was a welcome sight to the scattered population of the area.

BESTWOOD LODGE was built between 1862 and 1865. This photograph was taken shortly after.

BESTWOOD LODGE, designed by S.S. Tulon, and grounds. High society and royalty, including Edward VII and Queen Alexandra, Prince Leopold, Disraeli, Gladstone and Tennyson, paid many visits.

A FAMILY POSE FOR A PHOTOGRAPH in 1875.

TENANT FARMERS OF BESTWOOD, 1870.

BESTWOOD LODGE, the ballroom.

BESTWOOD LODGE, the hall.

SPENCER'S FARM, REDHILL. The path was the old road up to Bestwood Lodge until an offensive urinal at the White Hart forced the Duke of St Albans to negotiate a new entrance on Mansfield Road.

THE EASTERN ENTRANCE TO THE LODGE.

THE GARDENS.

A CRICKET GROUP on the most well-known of three cricket grounds in the parish.

THE INTERIOR OF ST EMMANUEL, built in 1869.

COLLIERS' PATH was the result of an agreement between the council and the duke for a right of way; the duke ensured his privacy with very high hedges.

WESTERN LODGE, BESTWOOD PARK, built in 1874.

ST MARK'S CHURCH, built in 1887, and the school erected for the children of the sixty-four families of the original village.

BENDIGO'S RING. This small clearing on the western side of Bestwood Park (now part of the housing estate) was the site where Bendigo, the famous Nottingham boxer, trained for his fights.

GLADEHILL, BESTWOOD, often confused with Bendigo's Ring. The whole area is now covered with residential building.

BESTWOOD COLLIERY. first sunk in 1871, closed in 1967. This photograph is one of a set of educational cards used in schools.

THE WATERWORKS on Mansfield Road at Leapool, built between 1871 and 1874.

THE BESTWOOD IRON AND COAL COMPANY, one of the duke's assets. It was opened in 1877 and closed in 1928.

WHEN THE ARMY WAS STATIONED HERE a review was held in 1966. The East Midland District of the Army finally left in March 1973.

For Investment, Capital Appreciation, Housing and Industrial Development.

NOTTINGHAM

896 ACRES IN THE BOROUGH BOUNDARY.

ARNOLD, BASFORD and BULWELL are adjacent.

ABOUT 6 MILES OF IMPORTANT MAIN AND ESTATE ROAD FRONTAGES.

ADJOINING RECENT AND RAPID DEVELOPMENT.   Fine Accessibility by Rail and Road.

AS A WHOLE, IN BLOCKS OR IN LOTS.   FREEHOLD.

The Important, Valuable and Compact Residential, Agricultural and Building Property

THE

BESTWOOD ESTATE

embracing

The Well-known Mansion BESTWOOD LODGE

Occupying the site of a former Royal Hunting Lodge

(as a Lot with 61 or 121 Acres)

containing :

Fine Hall, 3 Reception Rooms, Ball Room, Billiards Room, Conservatory, Gun Room, 19 Principal Bed and Dressing Rooms, 17 Secondary and Servants' Bed Rooms, 9 Bath Rooms, Excellent Offices.   All Services.

LOVELY GROUNDS and the BESTWOOD KITCHEN GARDENS

also

15 CHOICE FARMS

ranging from 31 to 357 Acres, offering great scope for capital appreciation.

IMPORTANT SELECTED COMMERCIAL AND SHOP SITES

OVER 500 ACRES OF BUILDING LAND

in parcels from 5 to 109 Acres, adjoining recent development within the City Boundary.

BEAUTIFUL WOODED SITES IN BESTWOOD PARK AND THE BIG WOOD

Large Areas of Valuable Mixed Timber and Pitwoods.

also

SECONDARY RESIDENCE,   24 HOUSES & COTTAGES,   ACCOMMODATION LANDS,
CRICKET GROUND,   COLLIERY SIDINGS

There are believed to be Valuable and EXTENSIVE SAND DEPOSITS

in all about

3,485 ACRES

Producing at present a Gross Income (excluding Lands in Hand) of about £3,340 per annum.

Which will be offered for Sale by Auction (unless sold privately meanwhile) by Messrs.

JOHN D. WOOD & CO.

At THE BLACK BOY HOTEL, NOTTINGHAM,

On MONDAY, 10th JUNE, 1940,

in two sessions, at 11 a.m. and 2 p.m.

Auctioneers : Messrs. JOHN D. WOOD & CO., 23, Berkeley Square, London, W.1 (*Tel. Mayfair 6341—10 lines*).
Land Agents and Surveyors : Messrs. BERNARD THORPE & PARTNERS, 32, Millbank, Westminster, London, S.W.1.
(*Tel. Victoria 3012—5 lines*).
Emergency Address : Effingham Park Estate Office, North Lodge, Copthorne, Crawley, Sussex.
(*Tel. Copthorne 524(5)*).

Solicitors : Messrs. HOPGOOD, MILLS & LONSDALE, 11, New Square, Lincoln's Inn, London, W.C.2.

Ward & Foxlow, Ltd., Printers, Harcourt Street, W.1.

THE END.

ACKNOWLEDGEMENTS

Thanks to the Nottinghamshire Archives Office, High Pavement; The Department of Local Studies, Central Library; Janet McKellar and the *Post*, and Universal Office Supplies, all of Nottingham.

All the illustrations have been collected by me and I would like to thank the library at Arnold and the people who have freely given me permission to reproduce. A special thank you must go to Pam Punter of Mapperley for typing, checking and having patience with the author.

Thanks, also, to Mrs Doune-Cooper, Mrs Edwards, Mrs Ashley Arlington, J. Tanner, T. Fry, R. Iliffe, G.H.F. Atkin, Betty Blankley, Beattie Barrow, A. Casterton, H. Cave, all local worthies, as well as Shiela Hodson-Kimmel of Missouri, USA, Mrs H. Pitt-Clarke of Ipsden, G. Oldfield of West Bridgford, D. Ottewell of Nuthall, Mr and Mrs T.E. Parr of Woodborough and Mrs Ward.

Finally, I would like to apologize to anyone whose name I have unintentionally missed.